Co- Parenting

Under Spiritual

Warfare:

High Conflict

By: Tonii Blount

Contents

"For we wrestle not against flesh and blood,
but against principalities, against powers,
against the rulers of the darkness of this world,
against spiritual wickedness in high places."

(Ephesians 6:12 KJV)

Introduction

One day I was riding with my babies, and my oldest asked me a very puzzling question.

"Mommy," she said, "what's the scariest thing that you've had to do?"

For a moment, I was shocked and lost for words. I wasn't expecting this from my ten-year-old. I had to ask her for time to think about the question because it sent me into deep reflection.

The truth is, from childhood to adulthood, I had been through a lot. I had seen a lot. But there was one mountain that I had to face — and am still climbing — that only God could help me navigate.

That mountain was co-parenting.

Having a co-parenting relationship centered on the well-being of the children from both sides is a beautiful thing. But if you are currently dealing with a high-conflict co-parenting dynamic, I urge you to truly consider every word that you read today.

I want to challenge you to shift your perspective — from surface-level reactions to spiritual awareness.

If you have made it this far, I can assure you that you are seeking answers.

You want what's best for your children, but you do not feel your best self, given the circumstances. You are tired of periods of confusion. You need guidance. You are doing all you can to co-parent logically, yet you feel attacked from every angle.

You want your peace back.

The problem is this: you are putting all your time into fighting physically and not enough time tackling the spiritual.

"I have given you authority to trample on snakes and scorpions and to overcome all the power of the enemy; nothing will harm you." *(Luke 10:19 NIV)*

Eye Opener

The reality of spiritual warfare is undeniable, but recognizing its presence requires vision that only God can provide.

Ephesians 6:12 specifically reveals the identity of the enemy we face daily. There are several situations and circumstances commonly classified as spiritual attacks — and high-conflict co-parenting should be included among them.

In 2023, I knew I had to make a decision: I needed to prioritize my spiritual growth and deepen my relationship with Christ.

Previously, my connection with faith was sporadic. My prayer life was nonexistent. I could no longer ignore the tugging on my heart. I recognized that I needed to build a solid foundation with God — and I am still on that journey today.

During that season, I went through a life-altering experience. I could sense God's guidance in my life. As the saying goes, I was "on fire for Christ."

My mindset shifted.

My thought process matured.

My self-awareness has deepened.

God showed me my true character. He also opened my eyes to the reality around me — including the spiritual warfare I was encountering.

"But whenever anyone turns to the Lord, the veil is taken away."
 (2 Corinthians 3:16 NIV)

The state of my co-parenting relationship was at the top of the list.

To face this challenge, I had to learn how to pray and fast. Trusting God was no longer optional — it was necessary. I leaned on Him for guidance, comfort, discernment, and strength.

God also revealed something important to me: my experience was not unique.

Many individuals were facing spiritual attacks in this area, often without realizing it.

"What has been will be again, what has been done will be done again; there is nothing new under the sun." *(Ecclesiastes 1:9 NIV)*

Personal stories about struggling with co-parenting began to surface. Yet most of them were not viewed through spiritual lenses.

And that is where perspectives must shift.

Reflection: Seeing Beyond the Surface

Take a moment to reflect honestly.

1. Have I been viewing my co-parenting struggle purely as a personality conflict — or as a spiritual battle?

2. When was the last time I intentionally invited God into this specific area of my life?

3. What would change if I approached this situation spiritually instead of emotionally?

What Is High-Conflict Co-Parenting?

High-conflict co-parenting is a dynamic where constant conflict arises.

Intense disagreements and lack of cooperation have become the norm. Every attempt to co-parent seems to escalate rather than resolve. Communication feels strained, hostile, or unproductive.

Oftentimes, the children — and your desire for the other parent to remain involved — are used as pawns.

You may experience being demeaned, talked down to, or consistently disrespected. Attempts to remain child-focused are misinterpreted or weaponized. Boundaries are ignored. Clarification becomes confrontation.

Over time, this dynamic creates mental and emotional stress that feels inescapable.

When high-conflict co-parenting continues without resolution, it can lead to prolonged disputes, frequent litigation, and instability — impacting not only the parents involved, but the children as well.

High-conflict co-parenting is not simply disagreement.

It is a pattern.

And patterns require awareness before they can be addressed.

Reflection: Identifying the Pattern

Pause and examine your situation honestly.

1. Does my co-parenting dynamic reflect occasional conflict — or ongoing patterns?

2. How has this dynamic affected my emotional health?

3. How might it be affecting my children, even if they do not say it openly?

4. What boundaries have I attempted to establish? Have I maintained them consistently?

Tactics Used in High-Conflict Co-Parenting

Hostile Communication

Hostile communication is a form of verbal abuse intended to provoke harm, frustration, confusion, or intimidation.

It may include threats, insults, constant criticism, or degrading remarks. Over time, this creates strain in any co-parenting relationship and makes healthy communication nearly impossible.

Comments undermining your parenting abilities may become the central theme of every interaction. Your original reason for reaching out is often ignored. Instead, you are forced into a defensive position — clarifying false accusations and correcting misrepresentations.

Hostile communication may also involve speaking negatively about you to the children, with those remarks eventually being relayed back to you.

The goal is not resolution.

The goal is destabilization.

Lack of Cooperation While Demanding Control

A high-conflict co-parent may refuse cooperation unless it directly benefits them.

Finding common ground or mutually acceptable solutions becomes nearly impossible. Boundaries are consistently disregarded because they limit the other parent's ability to exert control.

This control may extend to:

- Your actions
- Your words
- Your time with your children
- Your parenting decisions

Threats of legal action are often used as a strategy — not necessarily for the children's benefit, but to establish dominance and authority.

In these dynamics, co-parenting becomes weaponized. Even custody agreements may be manipulated and used as leverage rather than structure.

Mental and Emotional Manipulation

"You're overreacting."

"Those boundaries aren't your ideas."

"Someone else is influencing you."

Standing up for yourself is reframed as aggression.

Prioritizing your children's needs is portrayed as exclusion.

Your feelings are dismissed.

Your concerns are minimized.

Your reality is questioned.

Over time, this manipulation distorts your sense of clarity and creates ongoing emotional instability. You begin to second-guess your judgment, your boundaries, and even your intentions.

Confusion becomes a tactic.

And uncertainty becomes the environment.

Blame Shifting

Blame shifting is a manipulative tactic used to avoid accountability.

You may be blamed for:

- The other parent's absence

- Their financial shortcomings

- Their emotional distance

- Their personal struggles

Engaging in the "blame game" only escalates the conflict further. Words are distorted. Intentions are reframed as attacks. Accountability is avoided.

Unfortunately, children may also be drawn into this cycle — feeling as though they are responsible for the tension between parents.

The Bandwagon

In some cases, others are invited into the conflict.

Friends, family members, or significant others may participate in harassment, belittlement, or character attacks.

Their goal is to undermine your confidence and erode your credibility. These accusations often focus on personal matters unrelated to parenting, shifting the focus away from the children entirely.

What begins as co-parenting conflict expands into public pressure.

Parental Alienation

Parental alienation involves intentionally damaging a child's relationship with the other parent through manipulation, lies, or emotional coercion.

Negative narratives are introduced to create distance and distrust. Children may feel pressured to reject one parent to gain approval from the other.

In some cases, minor incidents are exaggerated or completely fabricated.

The child becomes emotionally divided — forced into loyalty

conflicts that were never meant to be theirs to carry.

Reflection: Recognizing the Tactics

Awareness brings clarity.

1. Which tactic have I experienced most frequently?

☐ Hostile Communication
☐ Control & Non-Cooperation
☐ Manipulation
☐ Blame Shifting
☐ Bandwagon
☐ Parental Alienation

2. How has this affected my mental or emotional health?

3. Have I unintentionally engaged in any of these behaviors myself?

4. What would a spiritually disciplined response look like instead?

How Does This Relate to Spiritual Warfare?

"The thief comes not, but for to steal, and to kill, and to destroy…"
(John 10:10 KJV)

The enemy's objective is clear: to steal, to kill, and to destroy as much of God's creation as possible.

Why?

Because he knows something that must remain hidden in order for his plan to succeed.

Satan knows he will never again have the opportunity to spend eternity with God. But he also knows that humanity has been granted that opportunity through the sacrifice of Jesus Christ — God's only Son.

"For God so loved the world, that he gave his only begotten
Son, that whosoever believeth in him should not perish,
 but have everlasting life."
(John 3:16 KJV)

As a result, the enemy works relentlessly to prevent individuals from experiencing God's presence, peace, and purpose in their lives.

He deceives.

He distracts.

He distorts.

He convinces you that the trial is the authority — when in reality, it is an attack.

Dealing with a high-conflict co-parent can create persistent mental and emotional strain. It can leave you in a constant state of distress. Many days may feel overwhelming, uncertain, and disorienting. You may begin to question your own judgment and decision-making.

Frustration.

Bitterness.

Resentment.

Regret.

Parents become angry.

Children begin to hurt.

But it is critical to look beyond the "trouble" parent and identify the real threat.

Your co-parent is not the ultimate enemy.

The enemy's primary goal is still to kill, steal, and destroy — and he accomplishes this by influencing individuals to fulfill his purpose, just as Jesus equips people to fulfill His.

In the same way Christ can place you in supportive environments, the enemy can surround you with individuals who unknowingly operate under spiritual influence.

And often, they are unaware.

This is why the battle must be recognized before it can be fought correctly.

Reflection: Identifying the Real Battle

Pause before continuing.

1. Have I been fighting a person — instead of recognizing a spiritual battle?

2. How has prolonged conflict affected my peace, focus, or faith?

3. What emotions have I allowed to take root in my heart?

- ☐ Bitterness
- ☐ Resentment
- ☐ Anger
- ☐ Fear
- ☐ Anxiety

4. What would change if I stopped personalizing every attack?

The Analogy

I often use the story of Adam and Eve to help others understand the enemy's tactics.

The fall in the garden introduced sin — the common denominator behind every trial and tribulation we face. It became the root of human struggle and the trigger for spiritual warfare. Suffering was never our original design.

From the beginning, Scripture describes the adversary as cunning — subtle and strategic. We are warned not to underestimate him.

"Now the serpent was more subtle than any beast of the field which the Lord God had made."
(Genesis 3:1 KJV)

The enemy cannot directly take you out. If he could, he would have done so already. Instead, he relies on indirect methods.

In the Garden, Adam was explicitly instructed not to eat from the tree of the knowledge of good and evil. Yet the serpent approached Eve — the one closely connected to Adam.

The enemy understood something critical: if he could deceive someone Adam loved and trusted, she could influence him to violate God's command.

Because Adam was the target.

Not Eve.

This is the revelation God gave to me:

The enemy often uses what is closest to you — relationships, responsibilities, and emotional attachments — as entry points.

Now shift your perspective to your co-parenting relationship.

This is not a temporary interaction. It is a lifelong connection — mental, emotional, physical, and even spiritual. And when that connection involves a high-conflict individual, the pressure intensifies.

The enemy knows you love your children deeply. He knows they are close to your heart. He also understands the stress that builds when your character is attacked, your integrity is questioned, and your limits are tested repeatedly.

So, distractions are introduced.

You become trapped in a cycle of defense.

Your mind stays preoccupied with predicting your co-parent's next move. Anxiety becomes constant. Emotional exhaustion becomes familiar.

Your focus on parenting weakens.

Your connection with God suffers.

You begin taking matters into your own hands.

And slowly, your responses drift away from alignment with God's Word.

This is how indirect warfare operates.

Reflection: What Is Being Used Against Me?

1. What relationship or emotional attachment feels most attacked in my life right now?

2. Have I become consumed with defending myself instead of guarding my peace?

3. How has anxiety affected my ability to parent effectively?

4. Where have I responded out of emotion rather than spiritual discipline?

Personal Testimony

"Whoever conceals their sins does not prosper,
 but the one who confesses and renounces them finds mercy."
(Proverbs 28:13 NIV)

I want to build a stronger connection with you as the reader, so I will take a moment of transparency.

The only way I can offer guidance on these issues is through my own revelation and experience.

In the beginning, I struggled deeply with my emotions. Fear. Anxiety. Frustration. Bitterness. Strife. They all surfaced at different times.

Despite my efforts to keep those emotions from affecting my co-parenting situation — which was already chaotic — I failed.

There were countless moments when I reacted out of anger. I was fully aware of the unforgiveness in my heart, yet I struggled to release it. And unforgiveness was one of the major reasons I remained bound.

Unforgiveness is heavy.

If you do not intentionally choose forgiveness — and prepare your heart to make it a pattern — high-conflict co-parenting will feel nearly impossible to navigate.

Establishing boundaries became a daily battle. When my self-control weakened, I compromised them.

I was highly sensitive to triggers, insults, and accusations. In response, I would send long paragraphs — overexplaining, defending, clarifying. I desperately wanted my intentions to be understood and respected.

I knew I needed a peaceful environment for myself and my children. I voiced it. I repeated it. Yet it felt consistently ignored.

Every time I was misrepresented, I fought back with words.

Every time negativity was spoken over my life, I rebuked it outwardly — but inwardly, I came into agreement with it because of the anger I carried.

I felt voiceless.

My confidence diminished.

I was drowning, fighting for respect.

In an attempt to maintain harmony, I began prioritizing the other parent's requests over my own needs. I convinced myself that accommodating more would create order in the chaos.

It did not.

Instead, I lacked stability. I lacked foundation. My mental well-being deteriorated.

I became desperate for solutions and began discussing my co-parenting struggles with anyone willing to listen. Though their intentions were good, their advice could not bring me peace.

Talking about the situation constantly made me physically sick. I was consumed by anger, confusion, and a deep sense of being lost.

But God.

In 2023, I made a conscious decision to take my walk with Christ seriously.

It was no longer about posting scriptures or occasionally acknowledging Him. It became a real relationship.

And everything began to shift.

The Lord started showing me myself within my circumstances. He revealed where I contributed to chaos. He exposed what needed refining. He showed me areas where I lacked strength.

The deeper I went into prayer, Scripture, and communion with my Heavenly Father, the heavier burdens began to fall away.

I realized something important:

I could no longer respond the same way.

Because more was required of me.

Reflection: Honest Self-Examination

Transparency invites transformation.

1. What emotion has controlled most of my responses in conflict?

☐ Anger
☐ Fear
☐ Pride
☐ Hurt
☐ Bitterness

2. Where have I compromised my own boundaries?

3. What unforgiveness am I still carrying?

4. What would change if I allowed God to refine me before I tried to fix the situation?

How Do I Spiritually Combat High-Conflict Co-Parenting?

"For the weapons of our warfare are not carnal, but mighty through God to the pulling down of strong holds."
(2 Corinthians 10:4 KJV)

1. Relationship

"I can't save you, but I can direct you to the One who can."

-Anonymous

To navigate a chaotic co-parenting relationship, you need direction from the Father.

So, before anything else, I must ask:

Do you have a personal relationship with Jesus?

If the answer is no, I invite you to surrender and accept Him into your heart right now.

Salvation Prayer

Father,

I repent of the things I have done wrong in my life. I realize now that I can no longer do life on my own. I ask that You come into my heart. I acknowledge You as my Lord and Savior. I ask that Your Holy Spirit lead me from this day forward.

In Jesus' name, Amen.

Choosing Christ means giving Him access to every area of your life — including your co-parenting challenges.

It means surrendering control.

It means trusting God to direct you.

As you walk with Christ, He reshapes your understanding. He refines your reactions. He strengthens your discipline.

High-conflict situations require spiritual empowerment — and that empowerment begins with relationship.

2. Prayer

Maintaining a prayer life is crucial when navigating difficult co-parenting dynamics.

Previously, when I struggled, I reached out to people for advice. I was searching for relief, validation, for answers. But those conversations rarely brought peace. I still had to face the conflict.

One day, I decided to bring everything to God.

No big words. No rehearsed speech. Just honesty.

I poured out my anger.

My frustration.

My confusion.

My fear.

There were tears. I felt broken. I wanted change but didn't know how to reach it.

"Come to me, all you who are weary and burdened,
and I will give you rest."
(Matthew 11:28 NIV)

After that prayer, something shifted.

I felt relief.

I felt clarity.

I felt peace.

That single prayer outweighed every venting conversation I had ever had.

It was a turning point.

The more I prayed, the more I returned to God instead of reacting to conflict.

Prayer began to change me before it changed my situation.

3. Self-Examination

The deeper I went into prayer, the more aware I became of my own behavior.

God began revealing:

- Where I lacked self-control
- Where pride was present

- Where unforgiveness still lingered

Anytime I responded incorrectly, I felt conviction — not shame, but correction.

Unforgiveness was a major trigger for me. I kept mental records of insults and accusations. I blamed myself for much of what I experienced. I even struggled to forgive myself for past behaviors.

But through prayer, I was freed from that prison.

Prayer taught me humility.

I released pride.

I released self-justification.

I released control.

My focus shifted from fixing my co-parent to refining myself.

4. Discipline & Boundaries

As my prayer life deepened, my reactions changed.

The need to be combative decreased.

I discovered strength in silence.

I learned that calmness produces clarity.

I began praying specifically for:

- The ability to set and maintain healthy boundaries
- Freedom from anxiety and worry
- Protection over my children
- A clean heart free from resentment

The calmer I became, the more logical my decisions were.

God showed me how anger had clouded my judgment.

Spiritual discipline replaced emotional reaction.

5. Perspective Shift

Prayer did not immediately remove the conflict.

But it changed how I viewed it.

I began to see beyond the physical behavior into the spiritual

influence behind it. And that changed everything.

Reflection: Spiritual Discipline Inventory

Be honest with yourself.

1. Do I pray before I respond — or after I react?

☐ Before
☐ After
☐ Rarely

2. What area do I struggle with most?

☐ Forgiveness
☐ Pride
☐ Anxiety
☐ Boundary-setting
☐ Emotional reactivity

3. Have I truly surrendered control of this situation to God?

4. What would spiritual discipline look like in my next conflict interaction?

6. God's Word

"For the word of God is alive and active. Sharper than any double-edged sword…"
(Hebrews 4:12 NIV)

God's Word is the blueprint for every situation we face.

Through Scripture, we gain knowledge.

Through Scripture, we gain wisdom.

Through Scripture, we gain confidence to endure.

When high-conflict co-parenting feels overwhelming, God's Word becomes both anchor and weapon.

Below are the passages that strengthened me along the way.

Trusting God

Psalm 55:22

"Cast your cares on the Lord and he will sustain you;
 he will never let the righteous be shaken."

This scripture reminds you to release what you cannot control.

It encourages trust over panic.

Dependence over self-reliance.

God sustains you — even when the situation does not immediately change.

2 Chronicles 20:15

"Do not be afraid or discouraged because of this vast army. For the battle is not yours, but God's."

High-conflict situations often feel like a "vast army."

But this verse is a reminder:

You are not fighting alone.

You are not fighting in your own strength.

Victory belongs to God.

Seeking Peace & Letting Go of Hurt

Romans 12:18

"If possible, as far as it depends on you, live at peace with everyone."

Notice the instruction: *as far as it depends on you.*

You cannot control the other parent.

But you can control your words.

Your tone.

Your response.

Peace becomes your responsibility — not their permission.

Proverbs 15:18

"A hot-tempered person stirs up conflict,
 but the one who is patient calms a quarrel."

Anger escalates.

Patience stabilizes.

In moments of conflict, slow down before responding.

Reflection often prevents regret.

Weapons to Fight Against Spiritual Attacks

Ephesians 6:11

"Put on the whole armor of God, that ye may be able to stand against the schemes of the devil."

Spiritual protection is not optional in high-conflict dynamics.

The armor includes:

- Belt of Truth
- Breastplate of Righteousness
- Shield of Faith
- Helmet of Salvation
- Sword of the Spirit
- Shoes of Peace

God equips you to stand — not react.

2 Corinthians 10:4

"For the weapons of our warfare are not of the flesh but have divine power to destroy strongholds."

Strongholds are mental, emotional, and spiritual patterns that

feel immovable.

High-conflict co-parenting can become a stronghold if left

unchecked.

But spiritual battles require spiritual tools:

Prayer.

Faith.

Fasting.

Obedience.

Seeking Wisdom and Discernment

James 1:5

"If any of you lack wisdom, you should ask God, who gives generously to all without finding fault, and it will be given to you."

Wisdom in high-conflict co-parenting looks like:

- Prioritizing your children's well-being
- Setting firm boundaries
- Communicating briefly and factually
- Disengaging from unnecessary drama
- Practicing self-care

Wisdom also requires self-examination.

Ask God to search your heart before correcting someone

else's behavior.

God's Protection

Deuteronomy 31:8

"The Lord himself goes before you and will be with you; he will never leave you nor forsake you. Do not be afraid; do not be discouraged."

This is reassurance.

God does not observe from a distance — He goes before you.

Even in conflict, you do not have to operate in fear.

Trust replaces anxiety.

Faith replaces panic.

He will not fail you.

Reflection: Applying the Word

Choose one scripture from this section that speaks directly to your situation.

Scripture: ____

1. How can I apply this verse practically this week?

2. What behavior must I surrender to walk in obedience?

3. Am I relying more on emotion or on Scripture?

Conclusion

Co-parenting within a high-conflict dynamic is not merely a relational challenge — it is a spiritual battlefield.

It requires prayer.

It requires discernment.

It requires obedience to God's Word.

When conflict escalates, the call is not to retaliate. The call is to stand firm — in truth, in righteousness, and in peace.

Through prayer, healthy boundaries, and a refusal to partner with chaos or manipulation, co-parenting shifts from reaction to spiritual stewardship.

Even when the other parent remains uncooperative, faith anchors your heart in God's justice and protection.

By placing yourself and your children under continual prayer…

By modeling Christ-like restraint…

By trusting the Lord as your defender and guide…

You become the faithful parent who walks in obedience rather than fear.

Peace becomes intentional.

It is no longer dependent on circumstances — it is rooted in God's promises.

And in this way, co-parenting — though difficult — can glorify God, safeguard your children, and confirm that light ultimately overcomes darkness.

Final Reflection: The Parent I Choose to Be

Before closing this book, pause and reflect.

1. What spiritual posture will I commit to moving forward?

2. What behavior must end today?

3. What kind of emotional environment do I want my children to remember about my home?

Bonus: Personal Commitment

Today, I choose to:

- ☐ Pray before reacting
- ☐ Maintain boundaries
- ☐ Protect my peace
- ☐ Prioritize my children's emotional safety
- ☐ Trust God with what I cannot control

Signature: _______________________________

Date: _______________________________

Closing Prayer

Father,

I lift up my sister and my brother who took the time to read these pages and seek deeper understanding of their situation.

Strengthen them along their co-parenting journey.

Break the stronghold of high-conflict co-parenting.

Grant them discernment to see beyond the visible attacks and recognize the spiritual battle at hand. Give them discipline to respond with wisdom rather than emotion. Fill their hearts with the grace to forgive — even when forgiveness feels undeserved.

Cover their children in peace. Guard their homes with Your protection. Replace chaos with clarity and fear with faith.

Let their obedience produce stability. Let their restraint produce strength. Let their faith produce victory.

In Jesus' name we pray,
Amen.